D0462866

A TEEN
GUIDE
TO

INVESTING

INVESTMENT
OPTIONS FOR TEENS

TAMMY
GAGNE

Mitchell Lane
PUBLISHERS

P.O. Box 196
Hockessin, DE 19707
www.mitchelllane.com

A TEEN GUIDE TO INVESTING

Investment Options for Teens
A Teen Guide to Buying Stocks
A Dividend Stock Strategy for Teens
A Teen Guide to Buying Bonds
A Teen Guide to Buying Mutual Funds
A Teen Guide to Safe-Haven Savings

Copyright © 2014 by Mitchell Lane Publishers

Printing 2 3 4 5 6 7 8 9

Disclaimer: Mitchell Lane Publishers is not a securities advisor. The views here belong solely to the author and should not be used or considered as investment advice. Individuals must determine the suitability for their own situation and perform their own due diligence before making any investment.

Library of Congress
Cataloging-in-Publication Data
Gagne, Tammy.
  Investment options for teens / by Tammy Gagne.
      pages cm. — (A teen guide to investing)
  Includes bibliographical references and index.
  Audience: Grade 7 to 8.
  ISBN 978-1-61228-540-5 (library bound)
  1. Investments—Juvenile literature. 2. Finance, Personal—Juvenile literature. I. Title.
  HG4521.G1754 2014
  332.60835—dc23
                                    2013017844

eBook ISBN: 9781612285412

PLB

Contents

Chapter 1
Do I Have Enough Money to Invest?
5

Chapter 2
Starting Small
13

Chapter 3
Planning for the Future
23

Chapter 4
Deciding Which Risks Are Worth Taking
31

Chapter 5
Saving for Retirement—Now?
37

Summary of Investment Options
43

Further Reading
44

On the Internet
44

Works Consulted
45

Glossary
46

Index
47

If you get a weekly allowance, you may have enough money to start investing.

CHAPTER 1

Do I Have Enough
MONEY TO INVEST?

You may think of investing as a topic for adults, perhaps just for wealthy ones. After all, as the saying goes, it takes money to make money. As a teenager, you might think that you don't have enough money to invest in anything bigger than a bicycle to get you to and from a part-time job. Even that bike might have to be a second-hand model in order to fall within your budget. Before you write off the idea of investing, though, consider just how much cash you actually have.

Do you receive an allowance? If your parents give you just $10 a week for doing chores around the house, then simple acts like unloading the dishwasher, walking the family dog, or mowing the lawn are earning you a total of $520 a year. Even if you spend half of this money, you will still have $260 to invest in a year's time. You may be surprised to know that this seemingly small sum is enough to buy stock in numerous companies—including Harley-Davidson, Intel, or Johnson & Johnson.

You may not be old enough to apply for a part-time job, but that doesn't mean you can't earn money. Odd jobs like babysitting, mowing lawns, or walking your neighbor's dogs could help you earn some extra cash for investing.

If you want to be able to invest even more, consider offering your dog-walking or lawn-mowing services to friends or neighbors for extra cash. Spending just a little time performing odd jobs or other part-time work can help you rake in a fair amount of cash to use for investments. According to Care.com, the going rate for babysitting in 2013 was between $7.50 and $12.50 per hour depending on the location. This means that if you babysit just four hours each week at the lowest rate, you are making about $128 a month. That adds up to $1,564 in a year! A part-time job that pays federal minimum wage and consists of just ten hours of work each week brings in more than $200 a month after taxes—and more than $3,000 in a year!

Investing your money instead of spending it all could help you attend the college of your dreams, buy a home as a young adult, or even enjoy some luxuries in life before you graduate from high school.

Maybe you would like to buy a car or another expensive item that your parents cannot or will not buy for you. Some parents make deals with teens to match whatever amount of money they can put aside on their own for big-ticket items. Saving and investing are the most practical ways for you to reach these goals.

Finally, consider windfalls. These are sums of money that you receive unexpectedly. A windfall can come from a beloved great-aunt who leaves you money in her will, or from a raffle ticket that you bought to support a local charity. You could also experience a windfall by selling some outgrown clothes or toys on eBay. Do your parents and relatives give you money on certain holidays? These gifts are another type of windfall. Some teens pledge to save at least half of every cash gift they receive. Why not invest that money to make the most of it?

Many parents begin teaching their kids about money by opening statement savings accounts for them. This is a good start, but these simple accounts earn next to nothing in interest. Interest is the amount of money that certain investments pay in exchange for the use of your money. Other types of investments may pay returns in other ways, such as dividends or capital gains. Your savings account is best used as a place to keep your money until you have enough to make your first investment. If you hang on to the cash, you may be tempted to spend it. It could also get lost or stolen. When you are ready to make your withdrawal, leave enough money in the account to keep it open, and start adding to it again to build capital for your next investment.

Before you can start investing, you must decide which investments are the smartest options for you. Investments fall into one of four categories: no risk, low risk, medium risk, or high risk. The risk of losing your money (or gaining less than you had hoped) is a possibility with virtually any type of investment, but this danger is greater with some investments than with others. You should never invest any amount of money that you cannot afford to lose unless there is absolutely no risk involved.

Hopefully your parents started saving for your college tuition when you were born. If not, though, it's never too late to start investing for this important expense. By opening a 529 or an ESA today, you can begin putting money away for your future. As long as you use the money for education costs, you also won't have to pay taxes on the interest it earns.

No-risk and low-risk investments include regular savings accounts, money market accounts, certificates of deposit (CDs), and savings bonds. Mutual funds, stocks with proven track records, college savings programs (such as 529s and ESAs), and individual retirement accounts (such as traditional and Roth IRAs) are typically considered medium-risk investments. High-risk investments include mutual funds that invest in sectors, or specific areas of the economy, such as energy and technology. Other high-risk options are small and mid-cap stocks, penny stocks, and commodities.

You might wonder why anyone would place money in investments that carry a risk of losing that money. The answer is that high-risk investments usually offer the possibility of a higher return on the investment. Low-risk investments may carry minimal risk, but they also offer very little in the way of rewards. Although the exact numbers are continually changing, in 2013 money kept in a typical statement savings account earned less than 1 percent in interest each year. A medium-risk mutual fund could offer a rate of about 9 percent. A high-risk investment in the right venture could earn profits of between 50 and 100 percent or more. Selecting one that will perform this well, however, isn't easy. It requires extensive knowledge and perhaps even more luck.

On the other hand, you might wonder why anyone would play it so safe as to earn only 1 percent on an investment. The answer is financial security. Many people would rather make a small amount of money consistently than make a large amount one year just to lose it all the

INVESTOR TRIVIA

You might not realize it, but buying gold and silver is one way to invest your money. The values of these commodities rise and fall in relation to the economy. In April 2013, a single ounce of gold was worth more than $1,500. Silver was worth much less, under $30 an ounce. From 2003 until 2013, gold earned investors more than 450 percent on their money and silver returned over 600 percent. People who bought these commodities when they were low made out better than many other investors. Still, no one can say for certain whether these investments will continue to increase in value.

next. For this reason, many people opt for low- or medium-risk investments.

Consider your financial goals when weighing the risks of different types of investments. Certainly, most people who invest hope to be successful at it, but financial goals involve more than simply making a load of cash. What do you plan to use this money for? When will you need it? What will happen if this investment doesn't perform the way you expect?

Many experts insist that the best time to opt for high-risk retirement investments is when a person is young. After all, if it doesn't work out, you still have decades to make more money and invest it in safer investments for a more successful outcome. A person who is planning to retire in the next ten years, on the other hand, doesn't have that same amount of time to make up for a costly mistake. If you are saving for college, you will need the funds within the next few years. Your parents may have been able to invest in a high-risk plan for you when you were a baby, but now that you are a teen, low- to medium-risk investments are more sensible options for college funds.

INVESTOR TRIVIA

The Future Investor Clubs of America (FICA) offers a special summer camp for young people interested in learning about investing. They learn about financial planning by playing board games, watching videos, and listening to guest speakers from some of the country's largest corporations. Students even get to go on field trips to various types of financial institutions such as the Federal Reserve Bank and the New York Stock Exchange.

401(k) plans are offered by employers to allow employees to invest for retirement. As a teenager, you can earn a lot more money over time by starting now.

Even if you invest with a reasonable amount of caution, you can still earn a decent return when you invest a large sum of cash. Imagine for a moment that your great-aunt left you $1 million in that will of hers. You could invest this money relatively conservatively and still make $90,000 a year on your money. Of course, most teens aren't lucky enough to inherit millions of dollars. That doesn't mean, however, that you can't make your own millions during your lifetime by working hard, doing a little research, and making some smart investment decisions.

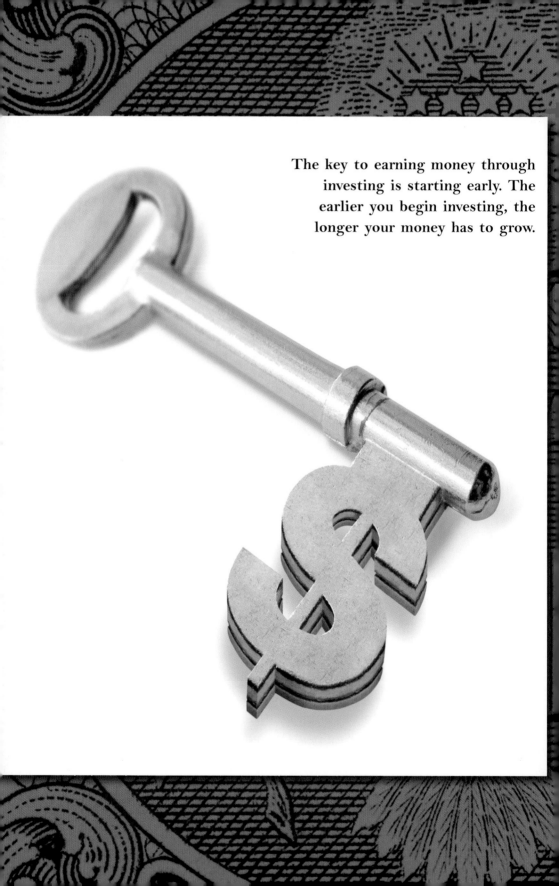

The key to earning money through investing is starting early. The earlier you begin investing, the longer your money has to grow.

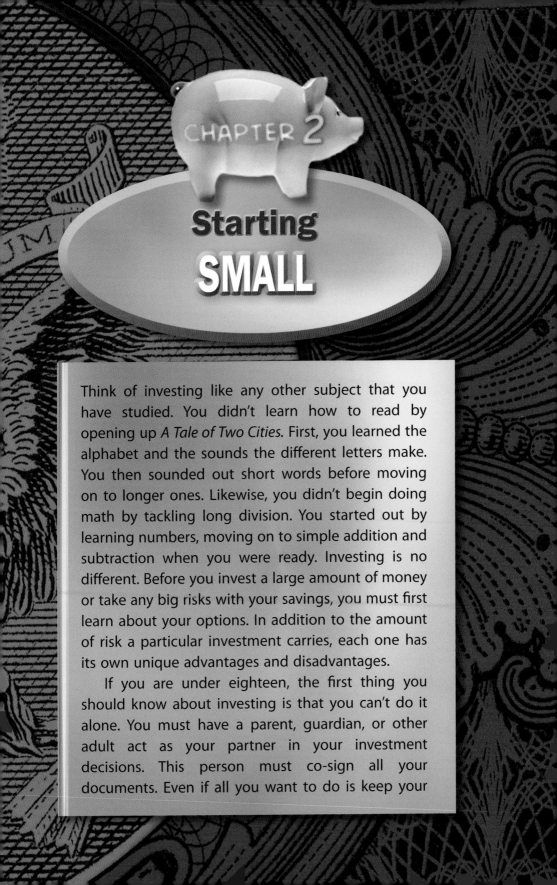

CHAPTER 2

Starting
SMALL

Think of investing like any other subject that you have studied. You didn't learn how to read by opening up *A Tale of Two Cities*. First, you learned the alphabet and the sounds the different letters make. You then sounded out short words before moving on to longer ones. Likewise, you didn't begin doing math by tackling long division. You started out by learning numbers, moving on to simple addition and subtraction when you were ready. Investing is no different. Before you invest a large amount of money or take any big risks with your savings, you must first learn about your options. In addition to the amount of risk a particular investment carries, each one has its own unique advantages and disadvantages.

If you are under eighteen, the first thing you should know about investing is that you can't do it alone. You must have a parent, guardian, or other adult act as your partner in your investment decisions. This person must co-sign all your documents. Even if all you want to do is keep your money in a regular savings account, you will need an adult to act as the custodian for the account. This is also true for purchasing mutual funds, stocks, and other investments.

While we're on the subject of that statement savings account, let's discuss the institution where you choose to establish this entry-level investment. Both banks and credit unions offer statement savings accounts, once called passbook savings. This was because in earlier years the balance was recorded in a small booklet. Customers would take their passbooks to the bank whenever they made deposits or withdrawals, and the tellers would record the transactions in this ledger. Today the majority of financial institutions have done away with

Spare change can add up, but you won't earn any interest on money you save at home.

passbooks. Instead they mail their customers monthly or quarterly statements that list their transactions and balance. Your monthly statements can even be sent to you electronically if you prefer.

Many banks charge fees for most, if not all, of their services. For example, some banks require a minimum balance for their statement accounts. If your balance falls below this amount at any point during the month, you will be charged a service fee. Some banks charge for making more than a certain number of withdrawals in a month. If you are being charged these fees, they could easily cancel out the interest you are earning, or even cause you to lose money.

Credit unions are known for charging very few, if any, fees for the same services. Doing business with a credit union instead of a bank may cost you less in more ways than one. Credit unions usually offer higher rates of interest on statement savings accounts. They also typically charge less interest on loans, which may be useful if you are investing your money to save for a down payment on a car or even a house of your own.

Although you probably won't make your first million from the interest on your statement savings, keeping some money in this type of account does have two major perks. One is that you don't need a lot of money to open the account. Even if you use a bank that requires a minimum balance, the amount is sometimes as low as $100. Credit unions may require no minimum balance at all. Perhaps an even greater benefit to a regular savings account is that the money you keep in it is always liquid. This means that you can withdraw your money with no penalties or waiting period.

If you are fortunate enough to have a large amount of money in the bank, consider keeping it in a money market account until you decide to invest it elsewhere. Also called a high-yield savings account, a money market account typically offers you a higher interest rate than regular savings accounts. Banks can afford to pay more interest on these accounts, because the accounts have higher minimum balances than savings accounts. Some credit unions offer money market accounts

INVESTOR TRIVIA

One way to keep your CD investments as liquid as possible is laddering. By spacing out your CDs or dividing your money among CDs of different lengths, your investments will mature at various times instead of all at once.

with no minimum balance, but they may only pay interest when the balance reaches a certain amount, such as $2,500. The amount of interest may increase when the balance reaches another level, for example $5,000. The Federal Reserve limits the number of withdrawals that can be made in a single month for both savings accounts and money market accounts.

The Federal Reserve guides the monetary policies of the United States. This organization's Board of Governors studies economic and financial conditions both inside and outside the country. The Board then uses this information to oversee the policies of national banks and other financial institutions.

When you first start investing, you may only have a small amount of money, so a statement savings account could be right for you. As your money grows, though, you'll want to move your money into investments that offer higher returns.

Once you have saved a certain amount of money, you may be ready to move on to a new type of investment. For many people this next step is a certificate of deposit. The minimum amount you need to invest varies depending on the financial institution. Some may require as little as $100; others ask for at least $1,000. A CD is a lot like a regular savings account. Just like a savings account, a CD is one of the safest investments available. Both are protected by the Federal Deposit Insurance Corporation (FDIC). This insurance covers each account holder for a total of up to $250,000 in each FDIC-insured bank. Always make sure that your banking institution is FDIC insured before opening any type of account.

The biggest differences between regular savings and CDs are the amount of interest that you can earn and the length of time you must leave your money in the investment. Certificates of deposit are available in a variety of terms. You may choose to invest in a three-, six-, or twelve-month CD, for example. You can even find CDs with terms of several years, but you must commit to the length of the investment at the beginning. When your CD reaches maturity, you may then decide to roll the money over into another CD right away or withdraw the money with the interest it has earned.

The more time you are willing to leave your money in the CD, the more interest it will pay. This amount is guaranteed, as long as you don't remove your money early. If you do, you will be charged a penalty, or early withdrawal fee. It is very important to read your contract carefully, as there is no maximum amount for a penalty. Usually, though, it's a portion of the interest you would make from the full investment period. The only risk of a CD is the possibility of paying this fee.

Money can wither away or grow by leaps and bounds depending on how you treat it. Keeping your money in a savings account with high fees will reduce your savings over time. Putting your cash in a safe investment with a reasonable interest rate and low fees, though, will leave you seeing green.

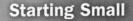
INVESTOR TRIVIA

The government limits the amount of savings bonds that a single person can buy. It will issue up to $10,000 worth of each series of savings bond per social security number per calendar year. There is one way around this rule, however. If you receive an IRS tax refund and would like to use it to buy more Series I savings bonds, you can do so. The limit for this additional purchase is $5,000.

CDs are often smarter investments than statement savings accounts for both long- and short-term savings. First, you are much less likely to spend money invested in a CD. Second, this money will earn more interest than cash left in a regular savings account. Even a high school senior who needs money for college will earn more interest by investing in a three- or six-month CD than by using statement savings for this purpose. The biggest disadvantage to CDs is that they still offer only a small return on your investment. Some people prefer a low return to the risk of losing money, though.

If you are interested in long-term savings, savings bonds are another very safe investment. Statement savings accounts and CDs provide banks with money to lend to other customers. When you buy a savings bond, you are investing in the United States government. Savings bonds can be purchased in any amount of $25 or more. Most people opt for round numbers like $100 or $500, but you can be as creative as you like when buying your bonds. Maybe you were born on May 12, 2003. If so, you could buy a savings bond for exactly $512.03 to honor this special date. You can redeem your bond any time after twelve months. If you do so within the first five years, though, you will lose three months' interest.

You've probably heard the tale of the tortoise and the hare. The moral of this story—slow and steady wins the race—can be applied to investing. By investing small amounts of money over time, you will increase your savings significantly over time. High-risk investments may offer the potential for big growth, but you could also lose most if not all of your money by going this route.

When calculating how much money you will make on savings bonds, keep in mind that interest compounds. This means it keeps adding to itself. When you buy a $100 savings bond, it will earn a certain amount of interest on this amount. Once the value has increased, the bond will begin earning interest on your original $100 investment as well as on whatever amount of interest your investment has already made. This continues for thirty years. Compounding interest makes a huge difference in the amount of money you can earn from any investment.

Savings bonds are available in two types: Series EE and Series I. Both start earning interest the first day of the month in which they are purchased, but the ways this interest is calculated are slightly different. Both series earn a fixed rate of interest, but Series I bonds also earn a variable semiannual inflation rate. This means that the rate changes based on the changing cost of goods in the economy, with the interest added twice a year. The amount is calculated in March and September of each year. Series I savings bonds usually pay a bit more interest than Series EE bonds, but this advantage is not a guarantee. Whenever an interest rate is variable, the amount can change for better or for worse. If you want to know exactly how much your investment will earn, the EE bond is the way to go. If you want the possibility to earn a bit more interest with a very small amount of risk, the I bond is a better choice.

Like so many other types of investments, savings bonds have changed somewhat over the years, but the basic idea remains the same. Until January 1, 2012, paper savings bonds could be purchased at most banks, credit unions, and other financial institutions. Today, buying a savings bond is an electronic transaction. You can purchase these bonds on the TreasuryDirect website at www.treasurydirect.gov.

If you have older series EE savings bonds, it is important to understand that savings bonds were once sold at half their face value. A $50 savings bond, for example, used to cost $25. It would be worth its face value once it reached maturity. Today savings bonds are sold at their face value. You purchase a $50 bond for $50, and it will never be worth any less than this amount. All savings bonds earn interest for thirty years. You don't have to cash them in at this time, but they will no longer earn interest past this point. All the interest from a savings bond is tax deferred. This means that you don't have to pay taxes on the money you earn until you redeem the bond. If you use the bond for education, though, there are certain tax advantages that will save you money.

One of the biggest financial mistakes you can make is keeping all your eggs in one basket.

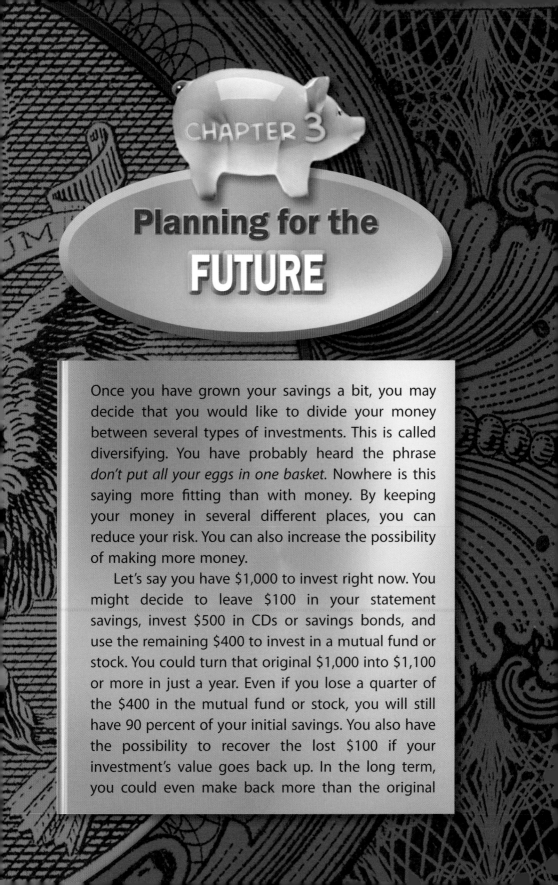

CHAPTER 3

Planning for the
FUTURE

Once you have grown your savings a bit, you may decide that you would like to divide your money between several types of investments. This is called diversifying. You have probably heard the phrase *don't put all your eggs in one basket*. Nowhere is this saying more fitting than with money. By keeping your money in several different places, you can reduce your risk. You can also increase the possibility of making more money.

Let's say you have $1,000 to invest right now. You might decide to leave $100 in your statement savings, invest $500 in CDs or savings bonds, and use the remaining $400 to invest in a mutual fund or stock. You could turn that original $1,000 into $1,100 or more in just a year. Even if you lose a quarter of the $400 in the mutual fund or stock, you will still have 90 percent of your initial savings. You also have the possibility to recover the lost $100 if your investment's value goes back up. In the long term, you could even make back more than the original

College is the first big expense you will face as a young adult. The more you save now, the less you will have to borrow to help pay for your education later.

$100 you lost. Just remember that you could also lose any or all of your original $400. It all depends on how the investment you choose performs.

Choosing medium-risk investments that will perform well can be tricky for new investors. No one, not even the smartest financial advisors, can predict the future. An expert can help you select the investments with the best potential, though. If you are ready for a small amount of risk, one of the best places to start is a college savings plan such as a 529 or an education savings account (ESA).

Named for Section 529 of the Internal Revenue Code, a 529 plan is a tax-free way to save for college. Putting money into a 529 plan is one of the best ways to diversify your college savings—without having to make decisions about individual investments. Each 529 college savings plan is made up of different types of investments including stocks,

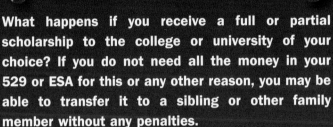

INVESTOR TRIVIA

What happens if you receive a full or partial scholarship to the college or university of your choice? If you do not need all the money in your 529 or ESA for this or any other reason, you may be able to transfer it to a sibling or other family member without any penalties.

mutual funds, and various types of bonds. The state that offers the plan chooses an investment management company to be responsible for selecting the investments that the plan will purchase. If you are very young when your 529 college savings plan is opened, most of the money will be invested in stocks. As you get older, a larger percentage of the money will be transferred from stocks into bonds and more liquid investments. As you enter your college years, most of the money will be in short-term investments with low risk. Stocks may still be included in the mix, but they usually make up no more than 20 percent of the total investment by this time.

Similar to a 529 college savings plan, a 529 prepaid tuition plan helps you prepare for your future education. It works in a very different way, however. With a 529 college savings plan, you invest your money with the goal of earning a return on your investment. You can then use the total amount for qualified expenses. These include tuition, room and board, books, computers (when necessary), and other mandatory fees. This type of plan carries a certain amount of risk. The money you invest can increase or decrease over time.

Through a 529 prepaid tuition plan, you lock in the current cost of tuition in your state at the time you purchase it. Investing in this plan

Investing in a 529 prepaid tuition plan is a lot like buying Forever stamps from the post office. Even if the cost of the stamps rises, the ones you buy will never expire. Likewise, the cost of attending your state's university may increase in the future, but the tuition you buy today will be waiting for you when you are ready to utilize it.

is a bit like buying the United States Postal Service's Forever stamps. When the USPS raises the price of stamps, all the stamps you purchased at the lower price will remain valid. Another person who buys stamps after the increase, though, will be charged the higher price for the same service.

Unlike a 529 college savings plan, the prepaid option doesn't involve risk. It guarantees a specific cost. The amount can vary depending on how many years of tuition are purchased at one time. It also only covers tuition and mandatory fees in most cases. Some plans do offer a room and board option that allows you to use excess funds for these purposes.

The biggest disadvantage to a prepaid plan is that it is only good in the state in which you purchase it, and not every state offers this type of plan. If you know for certain that you will be attending a specific college or university, this might not be a problem at all. If you don't know where you want to go to school, however, a prepaid plan will limit your options to in-state colleges and universities. A 529 college savings plan, on the other hand, can be used at any eligible educational institution in the country. Both types of 529 plans may involve certain fees, which vary by state.

An education savings account is another way to invest money for future schooling. Like a 529, an ESA places money in various types of investments. Once called an education IRA, an ESA also differs from a 529 in some important ways. One of the biggest differences is that an ESA limits the amount of money you can invest each year to $2,000. This is similar to the way that an individual retirement account (IRA) works. For investors who don't like the idea of their state making investing decisions for them, though, an ESA offers the flexibility for the account owner to decide exactly what to invest in. Some people prefer 529s to ESAs. Others might invest in an ESA until they reach their maximum contribution, and then invest the rest in a 529 plan.

With the rising cost of tuition, you could definitely have worse problems than having too much money set aside for your education. At the same time, it is smart to think about how much money you will need. If you plan to attend a small college, for instance, the cost will be far less than attending an Ivy League university. Any amount of money in your 529 or ESA that you do not use for school will be subject to a 10 percent tax penalty when you withdraw it. This amount will be in addition to the regular taxes you must pay on the money.

You can set up monthly contributions to both 529s and ESAs. Doing so is a great way to save as much money for college as possible without tying up all your money at once. You might open up a college savings plan with $1,000 and then add between $50 and $100 a month. Perhaps you could even make a deal with your parents in which they will add $50 for every $50 that you add yourself.

If you are smart about how you invest your money, you might be able to purchase your first car in cash, without an auto loan. This will save you even more money, since you won't have to pay interest to a bank for borrowing the money.

Although college savings plans offer useful tax advantages, you don't have to put all your savings into these types of investments. Placing some of your college money into other investments is yet another way to diversify your investment portfolio. You can pay for college, a car, or the down payment on a house with money made from CDs, savings bonds, mutual funds, or stocks. Having some money in other investments can also help you if you plan to open your own business after college.

Mutual funds are a little like college savings plans in the way the money is invested. These investments don't have to be used for

INVESTOR TRIVIA

A small increase in the amount of money you invest can make a big difference in your long-term savings. Increasing a $100 monthly investment by just $30 could increase the value of your investment by $10,000 over the course of eighteen years, assuming an average annual return of 5.5 percent.

education, however. And instead of your state making the decisions about your investments, you can choose the investment company that manages your mutual fund. When you put money into a mutual fund, you are one of many people who have done the same thing. The investment company takes the large sum of money from all its investors and buys stocks, bonds, and other types of securities that an individual investor wouldn't have enough money to buy on his or her own.

You may have heard the term 401(k). This is a tax-deferred retirement plan that a person can invest in through his or her employer. Mutual funds are often a part of 401(k)s, but mutual funds can also be purchased separately. Unlike college savings plans, mutual funds are not tax-free investments. You will also pay fees as an owner in a mutual fund. The amount depends on the fund you choose. Mutual funds aren't guaranteed by the companies that sell and manage them. None of this means that mutual funds aren't good investments. It simply means that it is important to select a mutual fund wisely. The same financial advisor who helped you set up your 529 may be able to recommend a good mutual fund if and when you are ready to make this type of additional investment.

Keeping all of your money in no- or low-risk investments can hold you back from the potential to make a lot of cash. Choosing safe investments for some (or even most) of your money may be smart, but if you play it too safe, your money won't have much room to grow.

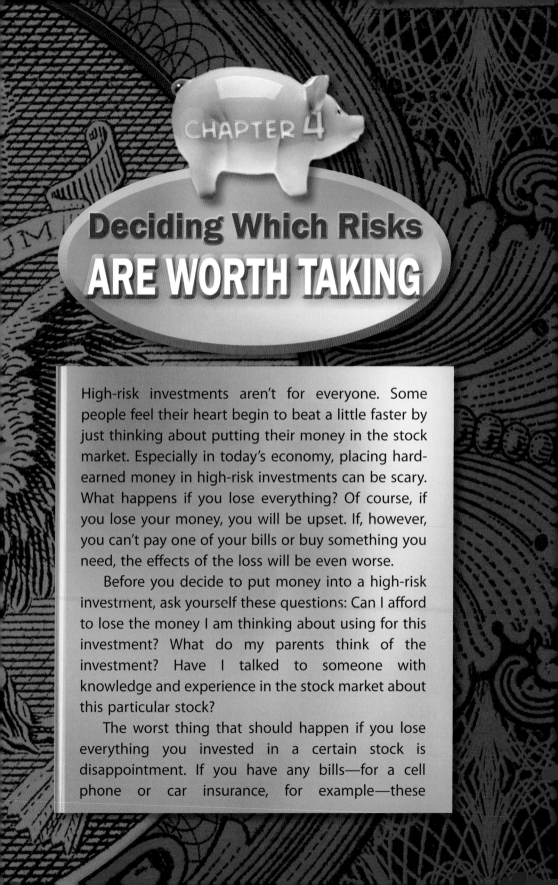

CHAPTER 4

Deciding Which Risks
ARE WORTH TAKING

High-risk investments aren't for everyone. Some people feel their heart begin to beat a little faster by just thinking about putting their money in the stock market. Especially in today's economy, placing hard-earned money in high-risk investments can be scary. What happens if you lose everything? Of course, if you lose your money, you will be upset. If, however, you can't pay one of your bills or buy something you need, the effects of the loss will be even worse.

Before you decide to put money into a high-risk investment, ask yourself these questions: Can I afford to lose the money I am thinking about using for this investment? What do my parents think of the investment? Have I talked to someone with knowledge and experience in the stock market about this particular stock?

The worst thing that should happen if you lose everything you invested in a certain stock is disappointment. If you have any bills—for a cell phone or car insurance, for example—these

INVESTOR TRIVIA

People who took a chance on Google when the company first offered stock to the public increased their investment by more than 900 percent over the next eight years. In 2004, the price per share was $85. By 2012, Google traded at a high of $767.65

obligations must be paid before you consider investing your money. This is true with all investments, but it is even more important in the case of a high-risk venture. If you pay your car insurance every September, you can place the money in a six-month CD towards the beginning of the year without any risk of not being able to pay your bill when the time comes. If you put the money into a stock, however, you could come up short.

Perhaps the money you are thinking about investing arrived inside a birthday card you received from your grandmother. While you may be comfortable placing this windfall in the stock market, your parents might not be as confident about the decision. It is important that you have your parents' support in your investment decisions. Even if they don't agree with your choices, they should approve your right to make them. At the very least you will need an adult to make a stock purchase, but many times your parents can also offer you the benefit of their own knowledge and experience about money. In some cases, they can even prevent you from making a huge mistake.

It is also smart to talk to a professional financial advisor before making decisions about stocks and other high-risk investments. No one knows for sure how the stock market will perform. Some very intelligent people have lost millions of dollars in the market. Sometimes you can learn from their mistakes. More often, though, the best thing you can do is take a calculated risk. This means doing as much research as you can, talking to an expert in the field, and making the decision that both you and your parents think is the best one. Crossing your fingers won't necessarily help, but it also can't hurt.

You can lessen your risk a bit by investing in a company that appears stable. This means that it has been around for a while and has grown a little at a time over the years. Take a look at the history of the company's stock. A slow, steady gain in the price per share over the years is a good sign. Don't worry if you also see some minor losses here and there. This is normal. What you want is a company that, despite a few ups and downs, has risen in value over time.

Buying stock is like buying a tiny piece of a company. This piece is called a share. If the shares in a particular company are being sold at $25, you would be able to buy twenty shares with $500. Each company has its own minimum investment, though. Different financial institutions also have their own minimum investment amounts. If the minimum investment is $1,000, you would have to invest this amount, buying forty shares.

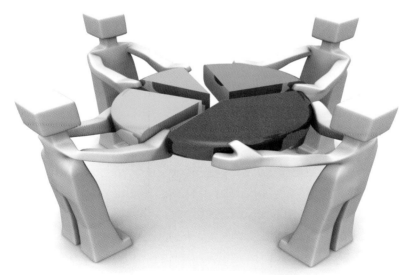

When you buy stock, you are purchasing a small piece of ownership, or a share, in that company.

Stock prices are always changing. As an investor you want to buy low and sell high. Say you spend that $1,000 on forty shares of stock in an athletic shoe company. If the share price goes up to $29 the next day, your investment is now worth $1,160. The next day, though, the price per share could drop to $21. This would mean your stock is now only worth $840. Most of the time stocks rise or fall just a small amount in a single day, but anything can happen. This is one of the scariest and also the most exciting things about the stock market.

When some people lose money in the stock market, they sell quickly to avoid additional losses. Sometimes holding on to the stock a little longer is the smarter decision for a couple of reasons. If you sell as soon as your stock suffers a loss, you will definitely lose money. If you wait, there is a good chance that the stock will go back up in value. It might reach the original price you paid for it; it might not. It all depends on the reason the stock value dropped and what happens to the company in the future. Again, no one can say for certain. The point where you think it wise to sell might be very different from the point where another investor thinks selling is the smart choice.

When a stock goes down, you could benefit from this loss if you choose to buy more shares at this lower price . . . if the price rebounds later.

Some stock purchase programs involve ongoing investments. You might invest $1,000 up front. In keeping with the previous example, this would buy forty shares. You could then invest $25 every month. If the price was still $25 the following month, you would gain one full share. If the price dropped to $12.50 a share in a month's time, you would be able to buy two additional shares. If the price rises again, you will gain value. There may also be months when $25 doesn't buy you a whole share. In this case, the money would purchase a partial share.

Many companies offer their stockholders quarterly dividends when the company makes enough money during a three-month period. The more money the company makes, the higher these dividends could be.

As the owner of the stock, you have the choice of receiving these dividends in cash or buying more stock with them through what is called a dividend reinvestment plan. In this way you can continue to purchase more stock whether you set up automatic monthly investments or not. The more shares you have, the more additional shares can be purchased with these returns on your investment.

You can always lose any or all of your money in the stock market. Nothing is guaranteed, but you can increase your chances of success by avoiding companies with a high risk of failure. Penny stocks are one example of a high-risk investment. These companies whose stocks are trading at ridiculously low prices may include both new businesses and companies that are in serious financial trouble. Some of these investments lure inexperienced investors with the potential of making a huge amount of money quickly. While it's true that the possibility for a huge return exists, there have been many cases of dishonest people providing false information about these stocks in order to increase demand and share prices. These people then sell their stock at a profit before prices return to their previously low levels. A trustworthy financial advisor can help you tell the difference between legitimately low-priced stocks and ones that are very likely to be a waste of your time.

INVESTOR TRIVIA

Many companies allow their workers to buy shares of stock in the company as part of their employee benefits programs. When employees own stock in the companies they work for, they care more about the business. This works out well for everyone involved. Perhaps the best part about buying stock this way, though, is that many companies offer stock to their employees at a discounted price.

Investing your money today could help finance your dreams for tomorrow. Would you like to retire before you turn forty, or travel around the world? If you make the right investment choices, virtually anything is possible.

CHAPTER 5

Saving for Retirement—
NOW?

Would you like to retire by the time you are fifty? How about forty? Does the idea of traveling around the world sound like something you'd like to do once you no longer have to go to work each day? Although these things may seem like they are a long time away, you can help make sure you have enough money for the things you dream about doing by starting to think about retirement savings now. If you start putting just a little money away for retirement now, it will have many years to grow— and grow. If you wait even ten years after graduating from college to start your retirement savings, your chances of retiring early will be much lower.

You have probably heard a lot of talk about Social Security in recent years. The Social Security Act was signed in 1935 as a way to set aside income for older Americans. When you begin working, the government takes money out of your paycheck for various taxes. One of these is the social security payroll tax. You pay into social security for as long as you work. Even

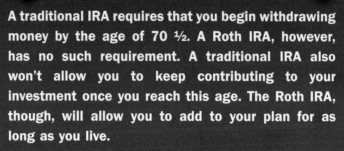

INVESTOR TRIVIA

A traditional IRA requires that you begin withdrawing money by the age of 70 ½. A Roth IRA, however, has no such requirement. A traditional IRA also won't allow you to keep contributing to your investment once you reach this age. The Roth IRA, though, will allow you to add to your plan for as long as you live.

if you only work part time, you are paying into this program. When you retire at age sixty-two or later, you get a certain amount of money each month called your social security retirement benefit.

Many people are very worried about the future of social security. Some experts are predicting that the money could be gone long before your generation is ready to retire. Many people who have paid into social security nearly all their lives could be left with only reduced benefits. The reasons for this problem are numerous and complicated, but they include a longer life expectancy, lower job wages, higher unemployment, and a rising cost of living. A long time ago many employers offered pensions. These retirement plans rewarded people for staying with the same company for a certain number of years. Today pensions are becoming less and less common. People need 401(k)s and other retirement plans in order to have enough money when the time for retirement arrives.

If you end up with a job that offers a 401(k) plan as a benefit, you should definitely take advantage of it. You can choose how much money you would like to put into this investment from every paycheck. Most employers will then match your investment by depositing an equal amount on your behalf. There is a maximum amount your employer will match, but not investing in your 401(k) is like throwing this money away.

If you don't have access to a 401(k), you should still start saving for retirement as early as possible. Perhaps one day you will have a job that offers this benefit. In the meantime, it is smart to think about opening an individual retirement account (IRA) for yourself. This type of investment plan is very similar to an education savings account, but the money is marked for retirement instead of schooling.

The biggest advantage to starting a 529 or an ESA when a child is very young is that it has plenty of time to grow. Another benefit is the ability to invest aggressively. Both of these advantages are also true of starting your retirement savings while you are still young. It may even be more applicable to retirement. A newborn baby has about eighteen years before he or she needs to pay for college.

It is important to understand the risks and benefits of each type of retirement investment in order to make the most of your savings.

You will most likely have more than forty years before you will need money from your retirement savings. High-risk investments do come with the possibility of failure, but they also have the potential to earn enormous returns over the course of decades.

Most plans allow you to start taking money out when you are 59 ½. Like college savings plans, IRAs charge penalties for money that is withdrawn early. There are exceptions, however. These include qualified

You might think of owning a home as something in the far future, but you can make this dream happen early by investing today. If you save for college with an IRA, you can use some of the money towards the down payment on your first house.

education costs, certain medical expenses, and money that will be used to purchase your first home. In this way, an IRA may be a smart investment for you now as well as for later. For example, if you have an ESA and have reached your annual contribution limit, you could open an IRA and continue to save money for college there. The best part is that this plan could be used for education if you need it, but can go towards a home purchase or your retirement if you don't end up needing it for college costs.

Just like college savings, IRAs are available in different forms. A traditional IRA allows you to invest pre-tax money. You can invest up to $5,500 a year into this investment plan without having to pay income taxes on the money. A 401(k) plan also works this way, but an employee can contribute up to $17,500 each year into one of these accounts. By investing pre-tax earnings into this investment, you are keeping (and growing) your money instead of paying taxes on it.

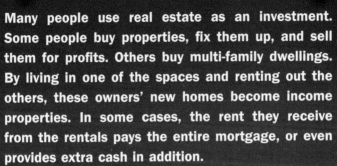

INVESTOR TRIVIA

Many people use real estate as an investment. Some people buy properties, fix them up, and sell them for profits. Others buy multi-family dwellings. By living in one of the spaces and renting out the others, these owners' new homes become income properties. In some cases, the rent they receive from the rentals pays the entire mortgage, or even provides extra cash in addition.

Another way to save money on taxes is by investing in a Roth IRA. This investment plan works much the same way as a traditional IRA. The difference is that you are not allowed to put pre-tax earnings into a Roth IRA. You're probably thinking why on earth would I choose a Roth IRA if I have to pay taxes on the money I put into it? The answer is because your tax savings with a Roth IRA comes when you collect your retirement savings. You won't pay a dime in income taxes on the money you earn from a Roth IRA. Some people would prefer to pay taxes sooner rather than later, believing that either the cost of taxes will go up, or that they will be in a higher income tax bracket when they retire. Either way, the only taxes you will pay on this retirement account are on the money you put into it. You won't pay any taxes on the money the investment has made over several decades. And this amount could be a sizeable sum.

One of the things that some people dislike about traditional IRAs—and even Roth IRAs—is the annual limit for the amount of money that can be invested in it. Although $5,500 may sound like a lot of money, think of how much more you could retire with if you could invest more than this each year into your retirement account. This is another reason for diversification. Once you hit the maximum amount on your IRA, you can put the excess money into other types of investments. It is wise to do so only after you have met the limits on your 401(k) or IRA.

Many young people dream of working for themselves in the future. Investing can help you save the money you need to open a business of your own.

If you end up opening a business of your own, there is another type of retirement plan that you should consider. It is called a SEP-IRA, which stands for simplified employee pension individual retirement account. This type of plan allows a small business owner to create and grow retirement savings with a higher investment limit than a traditional or Roth IRA. Instead of $5,500 a year, you can invest up to 25 percent (up to $51,000) of your income into this plan. Imagine that your business makes $40,000 the first year. You could invest $10,000 into your SEP-IRA. The more money you make, the more money you can invest for your future. If you have a small number of employees, you will be required to offer SEP-IRA plans to them. If, for example, the business pays you an additional 15 percent of your income in a SEP-IRA, you will have to offer the same benefit to your other employees as well.

You don't have to invest in an actual retirement plan to start saving for your retirement years now. If you create a diversified investment portfolio—and add to it consistently, you will be off to a great start for saving for the future. During your lifetime, you will experience good times and challenging times with money. A little planning, though, can make the difficult times easier to weather. It can also help you make the good times even better.

SUMMARY OF INVESTMENT OPTIONS

529

A 529 plan will help you grow your college savings through tax-free investing. Even if you can only invest $25 a month, you will be glad you did it when the time comes to pay your tuition bill. The sooner you start putting money away for your education, the more compound interest it will earn.

Certificates of Deposit (CD)

A CD is a great place for savings that you might need down the road. If you think you will need the cash in a year, opt for a 12-month CD. Won't need it for longer? Consider a three- or five-year CD instead. Choose the longest term that works for your circumstances, providing it offers you a higher interest rate. Just remember, there is a penalty for early withdrawal.

Individual Retirement Account (IRA)

The best time to start saving for retirement is while you are young. Doing so can make it possible for you to retire as early as possible. A regular IRA will allow you to invest pre-tax dollars. Since you probably fall into a low tax bracket at this point, however, a Roth IRA may be the smarter choice. This retirement savings plan does not give you any tax benefits now, but when you retire, you won't have to pay any taxes on the interest you earn through this investment.

Mutual Funds

When you invest in a 529 or an IRA, chances are good that part of your money is going into one or more mutual funds. You can also purchase these investments individually – once you have reached you're the annual contribution limit for your IRA, for example. It is smart to talk to a financial planner before investing in a mutual fund. He or she can help guide you to make the best possible choice.

Savings Bonds

You also won't earn much interest from savings bonds, but you also won't be risking your hard-earned money either. Savings bonds are among the safest investments in the market today. They are also a great way to diversify your investment portfolio. Choose either Series EE or Series I bonds at www.TreasuryDirect.gov.

Statement Savings

You won't earn much interest from a statement savings account, but it is a great starting point for your other investments. Use this account to keep your cash until you have enough to move into another investment, such as a CD. If you might be tempted to spend your cash before you reach a minimum investment amount, your money is safer in the bank. It will also earn a small bit of interest this way.

Stock

Stocks are among the riskiest type of investment, but they also offer enormous potential for growth. To keep your risk as low as possible, choose a company that has been around for a long time and has a proven track record. If you buy a growth stock, try to buy low and sell high. An income stock can earn you money through monthly or quarterly dividends. Even when this stock goes up in value, you may want to hold onto this investment, as your dividends are also likely to rise when the company does well.

Butler, Tamsen. *The Complete Guide to Personal Finance for Teenagers and College Students.* Ocala, FL: Atlantic Publishing Group, Inc., 2010.

Karchut, Wes, and Darby Karchut. *Money and Teens: Savvy Money Skills.* Colorado Springs, CO: Copper Square Studios, 2012.

Karlitz, Gail. *Growing Money: A Complete Investing Guide for Kids.* New York: Price Stern Sloan, 2010.

Kiyosaki, Robert T. *Rich Dad, Poor Dad for Teens: The Secrets About Money—That You Don't Learn in School!* New York: Warner Books, 2004.

On the Internet

MarketWatch: "Virtual Stock Exchange Games"

http://www.marketwatch.com/game/

The Motley Fool: "Teens and Their Money"

http://www.fool.com/teens/teens01.htm

TeenVestor

http://www.teenvestor.com/Investors/investor_introduction.htm

TreasuryDirect

http://www.treasurydirect.gov/indiv/indiv.htm

Works Consulted

Butler, Tamsen. The *Complete Guide to Personal Finance for Teenagers and College Students*. Ocala, FL: Atlantic Publishing Group, Inc., 2010.

FDIC. "Deposit Insurance Summary." January 1, 2013.
http://www.fdic.gov/deposit/deposits/dis/

Holmberg, Joshua, and David Bruzzese. *The Teen's Guide to Personal Finance*. Bloomington, IN: iUniverse, Inc., 2008.

Novack, Janet. "Will Social Security Be There For Your Retirement?" Forbes.com, April 23, 2012.
http://www.forbes.com/sites/janetnovack/2012/04/23/will-social-security-be-there-for-your-retirement/

Shore, Sandy. "Gold Prices Hit Lowest Level of the Year." Associated Press, May 9, 2012. http://www.huffingtonpost.com/2012/05/09/gold-prices-hit-year-low-_n_1503965.html

TreasuryDirect. http://www.treasurydirect.gov/tdhome.htm

US Securities and Exchange Commission. "An Introduction to 529 Plans." http://www.sec.gov/investor/pubs/intro529.htm

Waggoner, John. "Saving For College: Tips on 529 Plans, Scholarships." *USA Today,* March 12, 2012. http://usatoday30.usatoday.com/money/perfi/basics/story/2012-03-11/lifestages-saving-for-college/53444010/1

Wells Fargo. "Types of Bonds."
https://www.wellsfargo.com/investing/bonds/types

Zweig, Jason. "Did Your College Savings Plan Blow Up on You?" *The Wall Street Journal,* March 20, 2009.
http://www.sec.gov/investor/pubs/intro529.htm

capital (KAP-i-tl): money or property that can be used to generate more money

commodity (kuh-MOD-i-tee): a good that can be bought and sold and has no difference in quality from one provider to another

conservative (kuhn-SUR-vuh-tiv): purposefully moderate for the sake of being cautious

custodian (kuh-STOH-dee-uhn): an adult who acts as the guardian of an investment

deferred (dih-FURD): postponed or delayed until a certain time in the future

diversify (dih-VUR-suh-fahy): to invest one's money in many different types of investments in order to minimize risk

dividend (DIV-i-dend): a sum of money paid to shareholders of a company from that company's profits

ivy league (AHY-vee LEEG): a group of colleges in the northeastern United States with a long history and reputation of excellence

maturity (muh-CHOOR-i-tee): the time when an investment becomes due to be repaid to the investor

penalty (PEN-il-tee): a sum of money that is forfeited, for example, when a person withdraws money from an investment too early

portfolio (pawrt-FOH-lee-oh): the total investments owned by a person or group

security (si-KYOOR-i-tee): any of a number of types of investments, including stocks and bonds

term (TURM): a set period of time that something will last

allowance   4, 5

banks   14–15, 17, 19, 21

bonds   25, 29

certificates of deposit (CDs)   8, 16, 17-19, 23, 28, 32

college savings   6, 8, 10, 19, 21, 24–29, 39–40

   529 college savings plan   8, 24–25, 27, 39

   529 prepaid tuition plan   25–27

   education savings account (ESA)   8, 24, 25, 27, 39, 40

commodities   8, 9

   gold   9

   silver   9

compounding interest   20

capital gains   7

credit unions   14, 15–16, 21

custodians   14

diversification   23–24, 28, 41, 42

dividend reinvestment plan   35

dividends   7, 34–35

Federal Deposit Insurance Corporation (FDIC)   17

Federal Reserve Bank   10, 16

fees/penalties   15, 18, 25, 27, 29, 39

financial advisors   24, 29, 32, 35

Future Investor Clubs of America (FICA)   10

Google   32

income   37, 41, 42

inflation   21

interest   7, 8, 9, 14, 15, 16, 17–18, 19, 20–21, 28

laddering   16

maturity dates   16, 18, 21

minimum investment   15–17, 33

money market accounts   8, 15–16

mutual funds   8, 9, 14, 23, 25, 28–29

New York Stock Exchange   10

pensions   38

portfolio   28, 42

real estate   41

retirement   8, 10, 11, 36–42

retirement accounts   8, 11, 27, 29, 38-42

   401(k)s   11, 29, 38–39, 40, 41

   individual retirement accounts (IRAs)   8, 27, 38–42

   Roth IRAs   8, 38, 41, 42

   SEP-IRAs   42

risk   7–10, 13, 18, 19, 20, 21, 23–26, 30-35, 39

savings bonds   8, 19–21, 23, 28

   Series EE   21

   Series I   19, 21

Social Security   37–38

statement savings accounts   7, 8, 9, 14–15, 16, 17, 18, 19, 23

stocks   5, 8, 14, 23, 24, 25, 28, 29, 31, 32-35

   penny stocks   8, 35

   purchase programs   34

taxes   6, 8, 19, 21, 24, 27-28, 29, 37-38, 40–41

windfalls   7, 11, 32

About the
AUTHOR

Tammy Gagne has authored more than 75 books for both adults and children over the last decade. She has been investing for twice this time. In addition to managing her own portfolio, she has taught her teenage son about the details of his investments, enabling him to make some of his own decisions in this area. She believes that young people should know how money works, so their money can work for them instead of vice versa. When young people understand investing and feel in control of their finances, they get excited money. They also tend to have more of it.